This Too Shall Pass

Nora Domino

BookLeaf Publishing

India | USA | UK

Presentation by *BookLeaf Publishing*

Web: www.bookleafpub.com

E-mail: info@bookleafpub.com

ISBN: 978-93-5761-164-0

First edition 2022

DEDICATION

Dedicated to Anthony Patrick Domino and
Mary Catherine Habraken-Taylor

ACKNOWLEDGEMENT

Thank you Dad for all the laughs and life lessons you have taught me, you will forever remain my biggest inspiration.

Thank you Grandma for your kind words, encouragement, and beautiful soul. I carry your love in my heart forever.

PREFACE

I am writing this poetry book to help not only myself but others understand grief. My father passed away unexpectedly when I was in my sophomore year of high school. Not long after he passed, my only grandmother passed away as well. I still struggle with the "why" and "what." Why did this happen? Why were two amazing people plucked from this earth away from their loved ones? What do I do now?

I will always ask myself these questions, but my answers will change each time I ask myself, "why?" Grief changes a person's outlook of the world. A heart can turn bitter, especially in the beginning stages of grief. A heart can become numb. But eventually, it is healed, not completely, but just enough so that you can smile again.

"Above all else, guard your heart, for everything you do flows from it."
Proverbs 4:23

What Am I Feeling?

You are gone.
Gone.
Your heart has stopped,
And so has mine.
Where is the ache?
Where is the pain
That I am supposed to be feeling?
These fluorescent lights seem so dark,
Yet they still burn my eyes.
Or is it the tears that burn?
Or could it be the...
I don't know what hurts
But it hurts.
I know I feel something but it hasn't quite
Hit
Me
Yet

Day Two

I am tired.
My legs are iron rods
Buried deep into the earth.
I cannot get them free.
Each time I try,
They pull me down further
Into the cold, hard ground.
The walls are closing in
Threatening to turn me into an ancient fossil
That will never see the light of day

I thought that being close to nature
Meant peace and comfort.
But it is dark, and I am alone.
Whatever light you saw
It is nowhere to be found.
The light has left me
The only thing around me is shadows.
Are they shadows of you?

Heart Break Syndrome

There it is
The pain I was waiting for.
It took a while
But here it is.
Am I having a heart attack?
I feel the strings holding
My previously childlike heart together
Break, break, break.

Someone has cut these heartstrings
With a rusty knife.
They hadn't the decency
To remove them with a sharp blade.
No
It had to be dull.
They had to cut them slowly.
The pain isn't even comforting,
It's a poison
The only thing that could possibly save me,
Is you.

But you are gone
And all that is left
Is a stabbing pain in my heart
I am sure that I am
Feeling the same pain you felt
I'm so sorry you had to endure that
I would not wish this anguish
Upon my worst enemy

Sorry

Stop saying you are sorry
What are you sorry for?
You had nothing to do
With this tragedy
So stop saying sorry
You think those words
Are comforting
But they fill me with a fire of rage
Hot enough to burn Hell
The Devil himself would melt
If he were to get close enough to me

You understand?
YOU?
How?
There is a black hole in my heart that
Consumes every beautiful thing
That surrounds me
The whispers carried by the wind
Are now screams
The blooming flowers that dot the front lawn
Close their petals when I walk by

I am not permitted beauty so
You could not possibly understand

The ache that I feel
Do not compare your losses to mine
Never compare one loss to another
You know nothing
So don't say
"I'm sorry for your loss."

The Cherry Blossom Tree

I see you everywhere
Your smile is etched into the cherry blossom tree
That I once got stuck in as a child
I see you standing at the base of the tree
Smiling up at me as you say,
"You climbed up there, you can get down!"
When I made my way down
You were waiting for me

I climbed to the very top today
But when I looked down,
You weren't there
I realized that I couldn't make my way
Back down to the soft earth
Back to you.
The chilled December wind
Whispered what you once encouraged me
I could barely hear your voice
I was afraid if I left the tree
That I wouldn't hear your voice again

So I think I'll stay up here
Among the crooked branches and bare twigs
Just a little longer
Long enough so that I don't forget your voice

Soul

I have grown old
You would not know unless you
Reached into my soul
Pulled it out
And brought it up to the light
It has grown so small in your absence
I have tried to feed it
I have given it prayers
I have given it music
I have even tried to give it love
But it won't grow
It is barely there

What once was a flowering light
Is now withered and decayed
It has become wrinkled
I place it on a table
And stretch it out to make it bigger
But once I let go
It curls in on itself again
Like a cat dozing peacefully beside a fire
Its delicate arms reach out towards me
And I try
Oh I try
To lift it into my embrace

But I cannot reach it
What was once right in front of me
Is now eons away
I will try to bring it back to me

Faded

I have stopped counting the days
They blur together
As if someone took a wet brush
And blended all the vibrant colors
Of the painting that was once my life
And turned that work of art into a smeared mess
Of gray and black

Time will do that to a person
Blend all the colors together over the years
Until all you can see is black
Sometimes I try to paint a small blue
forget-me-not here
Or a yellow carnation there
But the paint runs together
The petals fall
And it all goes black

The details that were once so clear
Are faded
Am I even who I once was?
The biggest part of who I was
Was you
And your wisdom
How can I age if what little wisdom is left in me
Is from years ago?

Keys

For the first time
In a long time
I sat down on the cherrywood piano bench
And stared at the keys
All 88 of them
Sleek midnight black and smooth winter white
Each one of them a memory
A melody
Of you.
I figured if I pressed the right keys
In the right order
I would feel your presence
And so I began
Tentatively
Reluctantly

My hands shook
When I played those first few measures
The keys slipped beneath my fingers
Then I closed my eyes
And felt you next to me
Humming along
I held the notes down a little longer than I
should have
Just so I could keep you close to me

Those three minutes
Felt like three years
So when the song was over
I played it again
Six years have passed now
And you are still here

The song ended
I opened my eyes
And although I was back in the present
I treasured those extra six years
Whenever I need you,
I will play the song again
But never with my eyes open

A Symphony of Words

Your smile is etched into
The very core of my being
Thin lips spread across
Your rosy cheeks
Pure joy
Every smile you ever smiled
Radiated true happiness

A simple man
With simple wants and needs
But those simple things made you smile
You had your "isms"
That you uttered every hour

You had a new ism every month
"Ahhh baloney"
You would exclaim
When one of us complained
About the silliest thing
Suddenly, our worries no longer mattered
They were washed away by your
Nonchalant saying

You had a way with words
Your trademark isms
Were lessons tucked away
Waiting to be discovered
Between each remark

I recall upon them often
What was once an odyssey
To discover those lessons
Are clearer to me
Than a midsummer night sky

"I'll be back"
You once uttered
As you went to leave
Before you could close the door
I replied
"I'll be Beethoven"
You smiled wide
The corners of your lips
Spread across your cheeks
And repeated
"I'll be Bach"

We often said goodbye that way
I could not tell you
On your last night on earth
"I'll be Beethoven"
But I knew

In my heart
That you'd be Bach.

Less Than A Second

I have decided
That the pictures of you
Propped up along my dresser
Hurt to look at
So I picked them up
And began to put them away
When in my left hand
I felt something strange

A large object of some sort
Curled around my fingers
I flexed my hand and its' grip grew tighter
Opening my hand
I looked down to the floor
To see what it had been

When I couldn't find it
I realized it was your hand
You had held my hand
Just for a moment
As if to say
"Pictures are okay
I will always be near you
There's no need to put them away"

It was half a second that
I held your hand in mine
But you were there
You were truly there
Then you were gone

In less than a second
I felt everything
Joy, reassurance, comfort,
And then loss
All over again
But it didn't sting as much as it once had
Because you were there
You've always been

The Garden of Eden

I've left your comfort
Your foliage that protected me
The summer breezes
That whisked my worries away
I've been plucked
From the Garden of Eden
Into a cold
Desolate land

In the Summertime
I see glimpses of you
Oh Garden of Eden
I promise
I will return to
Your shade
And warmth
Garden of Eden
I carry you with me

Guilty Happiness

The smallest ray of light
Has come into my life
It has reached out its hand
And wiped away the tears
Cascading down my cheeks
I have tried to find this light
A comfort
Tried to recognize it as a glimmer of hope
But all I feel is guilt

How can I smile
Laugh
Enjoy my passions
If I cannot share them with you?
I can't permit myself that
Not yet
My heart hasn't shrunk enough
I need to feel all the pain
Before I permit myself
To feel all the love

The Storm

It pushes me in every direction
It shuts me away
In the darkest part of the universe
I have clawed my way out
And have been plunged
Back into the cold night

Sometimes
It cracks the door a little
And I can see what life could be like
Sometimes
It opens the window
Just enough
So that I can smell the Summer breeze
Feel the coolness
Caress my skin

These are just moments
That are quickly taken from me
Then back into the darkness I go
How long
Will I endure this endless cycle?

It tosses me like a ship
Caught in a hurricane out at sea

The eye of the storm opens
Bringing hope
Then it passes
And the ship is surrounded
By waves taller than Everest
No escape
I want off

The Mirror

When you look into the mirror
What do you see?
Do bloodshot eyes
And tear-stained cheeks
Stare back at you?
Does your smile not fit on
Your face just right?
Does it feel foreign to you?

When you look in the mirror
What do you want to see?
A genuine smile
Stretched across your face?
When you look into the mirror
What reaches out to you?
When you press your fingers
Against the cold glass
Will you cross the threshold
Between reality and fiction?

Should you break the mirror
Leaving the shards scattered
Across the floor
For your bare feet to be bloodied?

When you look in the mirror
What do you see?

My Companion

If only grief were a thing I could hold
I would be able to box it away
And put it
Into the darkest corner of my closet
And just forget about it
But grief is tattooed across my chest
Imprinted in my heart
I carry it with me every day
I cannot remove it so simply
And even if I could
Would I?

It is a part of me
That I am learning to love
So why throw away the things we can love?
Grief can be a part of me
And not become me
Some days it will consume me
Other days it will rest
And I can ignore it
Grief cannot be forgotten
And I suppose that's okay

The Cherry Blossom Tree: A Reprise

I climbed the cherry blossom tree today
To the very top
I let the leaves brush against my skin
I allowed the bees to flutter beside me
I sat on a branch
And looked down
The earth is not as far away as it once was

I still hear you calling
From the base of the tree
And though sadness touches me
It is just for a moment
I think today
I can climb down from the cherry blossom tree
And not fear the ground beneath my feet

I can gaze upon the cherry blossom tree
And remember you fondly
I can climb to the top

Hear your voice
And find safety upon the ground

Moments

In the moments that I can see you
So clearly
I can ignore the shadows
That I cast

In the moments that I feel your presence
I can welcome
The tears
That may follow

In the moments I hear your voice
I can allow them to wash over me
And rejoice at their beauty

In the moments you are there
I am alive again
When you leave
My heart still beats

Another Winter

Winter is not far away
I am afraid of what it will bring
Last winter you left
And all I was given was pain

I fear what gifts winter will give me
I expect more pain
What else could winter possibly offer?

All it can bring
Is gray clouds
Cold days and nights
And darkness
Winter will hide the stars
And a shadow will flood the earth

I expect winter to bring me
Nothing but loss

Loss

Loss is a funny word
It can be used in so many ways
It can be said in anger
"Have you lost your mind?"
It can be said in comfort
"You won't lose me."
But often
When the word loss is uttered
It means
Gone forever
"I have lost him."
You won't be able to find him
He is gone
Truly gone
If only loss always meant
Something could be found

Beauty

I have begun to permit myself beauty
I can turn my head up to the stars
And not feel darkness
But bask in their dim light

I have permitted myself beauty
Because I have realized
That without beauty
You would have never been in my life

You have shown me that beauty
Can be found everywhere
In memories, in songs
In the flowers that dot the lawn

I can permit myself beauty
Because beauty
Is what brought you to me
And I to you

This Too Shall Pass

This too shall pass
Every sob that escapes from my chest
Will not stop my heart
This too shall pass
When it seems like the world
Is caving in around me
This too shall pass

The heartbreak I may encounter
I can survive because
This too shall pass
I have fallen into darkness
But I have seen the light so
This too shall pass
I have endured the pain
Of losing you but
This too shall pass

Your words I will carry with me forever
I will call upon every time
You held me tight and told me
This too shall pass
I will come across many pains
In my life
But you have taught me

This too shall pass
And so it will